ECONOMY IN ACTION!

SAVING & INVESTING

BreAnn Rumsch
ABDO Publishing Company

visit us at
www.abdopublishing.com

Published by ABDO Publishing Company, PO Box 398166, Minneapolis, MN 55439. Copyright © 2013 by Abdo Consulting Group, Inc. International copyrights reserved in all countries. No part of this book may be reproduced in any form without written permission from the publisher. The Checkerboard Library™ is a trademark and logo of ABDO Publishing Company.

Printed in the United States of America, North Mankato, Minnesota.
052012
092012

 PRINTED ON RECYCLED PAPER

Cover Photo: iStockphoto
Interior Photos: Alamy p. 24; AP Images pp. 21, 22; Corbis pp. 7, 14–15; Getty Images pp. 5, 11, 17; Glow Images pp. 9, 13; Neil Klinepier p. 25; Thinkstock pp. 1, 6, 27; US National Archives and Records Administration p. 19

Editors: Megan M. Gunderson, Stephanie Hedlund
Art Direction: Neil Klinepier

Library of Congress Cataloging-in-Publication Data

Rumsch, BreAnn, 1981-
  Saving & investing / BreAnn Rumsch.
    p. cm. -- (Economy in action!)
  Includes indexes.
  ISBN 978-1-61783-490-5
  1. Investments--Juvenile literature. 2. Saving and investment--Juvenile literature. 3. Stocks--Juvenile literature. I. Title.
  HG4521.R86 2013
  339.4'3--dc23
                        2012018279

Contents

Managing Money

Have you ever earned money from babysitting or mowing the lawn? Have you been given money as a gift? What do you do with your money? Are you a saver or a spender? Or, are you an investor?

Spending money only takes an instant. Then, that money is gone. Saving and investing take patience. Both of these actions are important for financial health.

Let's take a closer look. Saving allows you to plan for future wants and needs. It also protects you when funds are limited. Investing involves some risk. But, it allows you to grow your wealth more quickly. Both methods count on you earning interest.

There are many options for managing your money. The right one for you depends on your short-term and long-term goals. So, keep reading to learn more about saving and investing!

Many Americans save less than they would like to. What do you do with your money?

Budgeting

One of the best tools for managing your money is a budget. A budget helps you see how much money you earn. It also shows you where money is spent. A budget helps you make a plan for your money, too. This may be setting money aside in savings, investing it, or both!

When you make your budget, it should include three basic areas. These are spending, giving, and saving. You can't avoid spending money. So, the money for everyday needs is your spending money.

Plan ahead for spending, giving, and saving. Divide your cash for these areas into three labeled jars, piggy banks, envelopes, or shoeboxes.

If you can't afford to give money to others, give your time instead!

When spending this money, you must learn to choose between needs and wants. Needs are things you must have to survive. For example, everyone needs shelter and food! Wants are everything else. It's okay to spend money on them. But make sure your needs are taken care of first.

Is helping others important to you? Setting money aside for giving allows you to help your place of worship or a charity. Maybe you care about helping an animal shelter. Helping others can feel good. So think about how you can put your money for giving to work.

Saving Cents

Let's not forget about the third area of your budget. Saving is an important skill to learn. It is the practice of choosing to *not* spend some of your money right away. Setting this money aside is known as paying yourself.

So learn to pay yourself first. This will make both you and your savings goals a financial **priority**. Soon, you won't even miss spending the money you are saving instead!

Sometimes saving means not getting everything you want when you want it. This delayed gratification is tough at first! But smart savers know a secret. By saving, they will be able to buy better or more items later.

Savings can help people make a large purchase, such as a house. Did your family recently go on a vacation? Did you receive nice gifts at the holidays? Savings may have allowed your family to do these special things.

Savings can also help during unexpected events. Have you heard the phrase "saving for a rainy day"? Losing your job can feel pretty rainy! So can dealing with a car repair. But knowing money is tucked away in savings can make these events less **stressful**.

Think of your life as a business. It has to make money to stay open and thrive! So pay yourself first.

Banking On It

Do you stash your cash in a piggy bank in your bedroom? Or do you have a bank account? Your money is safer in a real bank than in a piggy bank. When your money is in a bank, it is protected against loss. It's also less tempting to spend when money is out of reach!

Banks offer several ways to save your money. A savings account is meant specifically for saving money. Still, the money you deposit is usually available to take out whenever you wish.

Time deposit savings accounts work a little differently. Some limit when and how much money you can take out. Certificates of deposit (CDs) are one type of time deposit. Money in CDs is left to grow for a set amount of time.

A money market is yet another savings account option. Your money is invested in short-term loans. Those loans earn money, so your account grows more quickly.

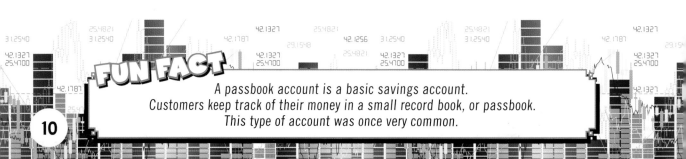

FUN FACT

A passbook account is a basic savings account.
Customers keep track of their money in a small record book, or passbook.
This type of account was once very common.

Are you saving up for new fishing gear? When you have enough money saved, you can take it out of your savings account and go shopping!

Interest, Indeed

There's another good reason to choose a savings account over a piggy bank. Money you save at the bank may grow. That's because some banks pay interest on savings accounts.

There are two types of interest. Simple interest is paid on your original **balance**. Compound interest can grow money much faster. It is paid on the balance and any earned interest.

Compound interest can mean some hard math! However, the Rule of 72 is an easy tool anyone can use. It can tell you how long it takes for compounding money to double.

Let's say you received $50 for your birthday. Now you want to save it. If the interest rate for your savings account is 5 percent, you will need to divide 5 into 72. The result is 14.4. This means your $50 will turn into $100 in just over 14 years!

As you can see, compound interest is great news to a saver. The longer you save your money, the faster it will grow.

FUN FACT

In the United States, savings accounts most commonly pay interest that is calculated daily.

RULE OF 72

72 ÷ INTEREST RATE = NUMBER OF YEARS TO DOUBLE

Year	Value (at 5%)
0	$50.00
1	$52.50
2	$55.13
3	$57.88
4	$60.78
5	$63.81
6	$67.00
7	$70.36
8	$73.87
9	$77.57
10	$81.44
11	$85.52
12	$89.79
13	$94.28
14	$99.00

The Rule of 72 can give you a general idea of how compound interest grows your money.

Interest also plays an important role in the economy. Businesses, governments, and consumers all borrow and lend money. Lenders charge borrowers interest for the use of their money.

Perhaps you want to buy a new snowboard. Your dad agrees to loan you $200. You agree to pay him back over one year with simple interest at 20 percent.

In this example, $200 is the **principal**. Simple interest is paid back a little at a time. But, it is only paid on the principal. The

Interest is not just for savers. It is also the price paid to lenders. Interest pays them for the service of borrowing their money.

total amount you would repay your dad is $240, or $200 plus 20 percent.

Now let's say your dad wants to be repaid over that year with compound interest at 20 percent. If the loan compounds daily, you will pay part of 20 percent interest 365 times.

Each time, you will pay a little more. This is because you are paying on the **principal** amount and the interest owed. In the end, you would owe your dad $244.27.

The $4.27 difference here may not seem large. However, compound interest is special. The larger the amount owed and the longer it compounds, the faster it grows.

In the case of a loan, compound interest works in the lender's favor. So if you have a **debt** to pay off, the faster the better!

Best to Invest?

Interest is especially important when it comes to investing. The interest paid on investments allows people to earn income from their existing money.

There are two main kinds of investments. Direct investments involve purchasing **real estate**, a business, or another kind of physical good. Indirect investments involve building financial **assets**. These include saving money or purchasing **securities**.

Investing is key to economic growth. But how does *not* spending help the economy? When you build wealth, there is more money to spend.

In turn, it becomes easier to get the goods and services you want. It it also easier to get more of what you want. So, growth leads to spending. This can raise a nation's **standard of living**.

Yet, to invest means putting your money at risk. Property and securities can lose value. So, you need to do some research before choosing to save or invest. Let's look closer at investing.

Working for a paycheck is the primary way to earn a living. What will you do with the money you earn?

To Market

You've probably heard of the stock market. It often gets a starring role in the news. But what is it? A stock market is a network for trading **securities**.

Back in 1929, the stock market crashed and the country fell into the **Great Depression**. Then in 1934, Congress passed the Securities Exchange Act. It improved trading practices.

The act also put the new Securities and Exchange Commission (SEC) in charge of securities laws. The SEC still protects people who invest their money.

But where does the trading happen? At a stock exchange! The New York Stock Exchange (NYSE) is located at the corner of Wall Street and Broad Street in New York City. Started in 1792, it is the oldest exchange in the United States.

FUN FACT

Nasdaq was created in 1971.
It is the oldest electronic stock market in the world. It lists stocks for technology companies. Trading takes place over a vast computer network.

In 2006, the NYSE merged with several other stock companies. This allowed trading to take place on the NYSE floor, electronically, and in Europe. The American Stock Exchange (Amex) became part of the NYSE in 2008.

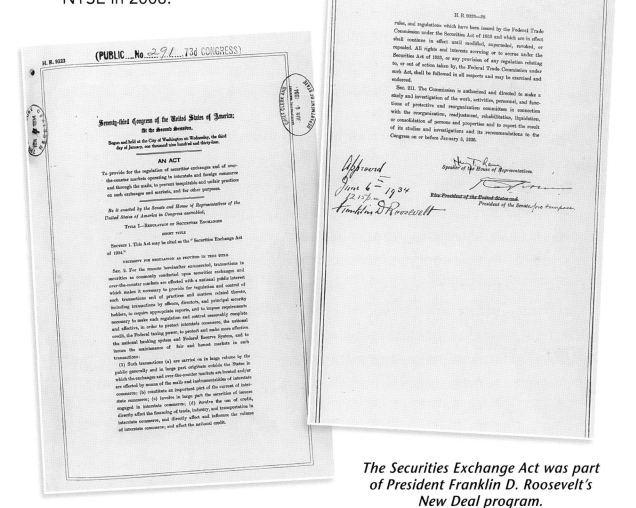

The Securities Exchange Act was part of President Franklin D. Roosevelt's New Deal program.

Stocks

At a stock exchange, only specific stocks, known as listed stocks, are available for trading. So what is stock anyway? It is a right of ownership in a **corporation**.

Stock is divided into shares, which can be sold. But the prices can change. When a business is growing, buyers want its stock. As more people buy more shares, the stock value increases. This causes its price to rise. The price may even grow greater than the purchase price. Then, shareholders could sell it for a profit!

Yet when a business or the economy is not doing well, the value of stock can drop. Some stockholders may sell shares. Others simply stop buying. So, the stock's price falls. Shareholders may have paid more than the current price for their shares. If they want to sell, they may take a loss.

But how do stock traders know how stock is performing? Several firms measure this information. The Dow Jones Industrial Average is one. It publishes an index that measures the level of American stock prices.

Standard & Poor **Corporation** (S&P) also publishes indexes. The most well known is the 500 Index. It measures the prices of stock for 500 companies. Their shares are traded on the NYSE.

BEAR OR BULL?

Stock prices rise and fall due to changes in the economy or unforeseen circumstances.

When business conditions are poor, more people want to sell than buy. This causes a bear market. Investors sell, hoping to buy the stock back at a cheaper price.

When business conditions are good, more people want to buy than sell. This creates a bull market. Investors buy, hoping to gain stock before it becomes more expensive.

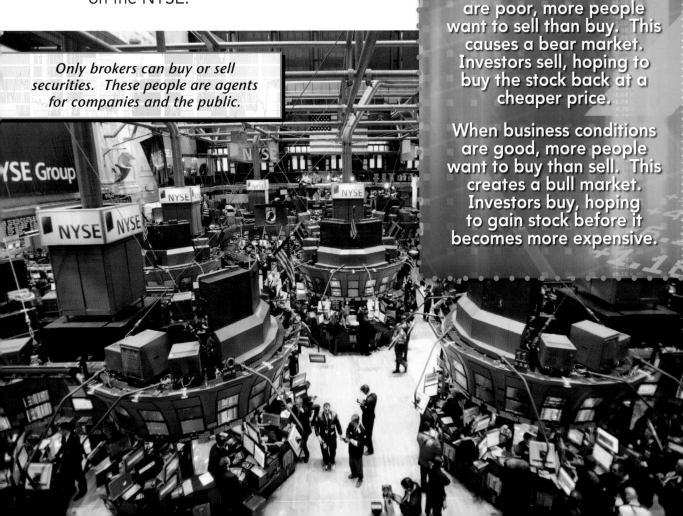

Only brokers can buy or sell securities. These people are agents for companies and the public.

Making Money

Once a company's stock is listed, how is money made? Through buying and selling! After shares have been purchased, investors hope they will earn capital gains or dividends.

Capital gains are earned when stock is sold for more than it was purchased for. Dividends are earned less directly. When a company earns a profit, it may choose to divide some of the money among the shares.

For example, let's say there are 100 shares of stock for a small company. The company earns a profit of $100,000. It decides to give half of this money

When a company issues stock for the first time, this is done in an initial public offering (IPO). Facebook launched its IPO on May 18, 2012. It was the second-largest IPO in history.

to those shares. That means each share would earn a dividend of $50,000 ÷ 100, or $500. If you owned 10 shares, your total dividend would be $500 x 10, or $5,000!

Prices change, but the number of shares available for trade does not. As the price of a stock increases, it may become too expensive for some investors. A stock split is a way for a company to bring down the share price for new investors.

In a 2-for-1 stock split, shareholders are given an additional share for every one owned. If a company had 10 million shares before a split, it will have 20 million shares after.

While the shares have doubled, the stock price will be half. So if the shares were originally worth $2 each, they will now be worth only $1.

After the split, the company's worth has not changed. Yet existing shareholders have gained shares! If the prices rise, they have more stock to trade with.

2-FOR-1 SPLIT

	Shares (millions)	Share Value	Total Value (millions)
BEFORE	10	$2	10 x $2 = $20
AFTER	20	$1	20 x $1 = $20

What Are Bonds?

There are other ways to invest, too. For example, bonds carry less risk than stocks do. A bond is a certificate given in exchange for money. It promises to pay back the money, with interest, at some future date.

There are several types of bonds. A certificate issued by a business is known as a corporate bond. People who buy them are considered creditors. This allows a business to raise money without increasing the number of owners.

Governments issue bonds to raise money, too. Federal, state, and local

Anyone can check the interest rates of stocks or bonds in local newspapers or online.

MUTUAL FUNDS

Mutual funds are companies that make a variety of investments and sell the shares. They can provide a low-risk way for people to make investments.

24

governments all issue **securities**. The funds raised are often used for public projects, such as dams and roads.

Government savings bonds are available as either EE or I bonds. They can be purchased for $25 or more and can be cashed after 12 months. However, they may earn interest for up to 30 years!

Treasury bills, or T-bills, are another type of government bond. T-bills can be purchased for at least $100. They are sold at a discount from the face value. They can be redeemed after 4, 13, 26, or 52 weeks. This is much faster than savings bonds!

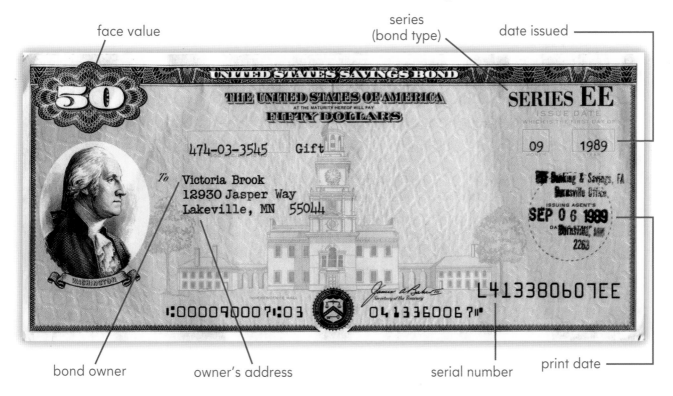

face value

series
(bond type)

date issued

bond owner

owner's address

serial number

print date

Risk to Reward

Economists often advise people not to put all their eggs in one basket. What exactly does that mean, anyway? It means that like life, the market can change without warning. Spreading your money out can protect you from trouble.

Money all in one place is like walking a tightrope. One wrong step and you're in trouble! But by using savings, stocks, and bonds together, you can worry less about a fall.

For example, savings accounts are low risk. This means they won't lose money. However, interest paid can be low. So, they are not the most powerful tool for growing your money.

Investing at a higher interest rate has more risk. But over time, the buying power of money goes down. Eventually, a secret stash of cash won't buy as much as when you put it there. But, growing your money with interest can help you stay ahead of **inflation**.

It is never too late to start saving and investing! Becoming a saver early in life will allow interest to work for you. When you are older, that savings will let you risk more when you invest.

FIVE STAGES OF INVESTING

1. Start a bank account.

2. Invest in bonds.

3. Invest in stocks or mutual funds on a regular, planned schedule.

4. Increase the variety of investments you have and keep your eye on balancing losses and gains.

5. Invest in high-risk, high-yield securities or collectibles.

Before you spend money, think about how it could work for you in the future. Will you save or invest it instead?

ECONOMIC EXERCISES

A GAME OF RISK

Look at the types of securities listed below. Write them down on a piece of paper. Order them from lowest to highest level of risk involved for an investor.

corporate bond

IPO

established stock

savings account

savings bond

mutual fund

money market

TREASURE HUNT

The US Treasury is holding about $16 billion in savings bonds no one has claimed. Use the Treasury Hunt Web site to find out if any belong to you!
www.treasuryhunt.gov

THE POWER OF COMPOUND INTEREST

Q: Which you would rather put in your savings account for 30 days? The choice is either $10,000 each day or a penny that doubles its value each day. Here's a hint. That penny is growing thanks to compound interest.

Day	$10,000.00	a penny
Day 1	$10,000.00	$0.01
Day 5	$50,000.00	$0.16
Day 10	$100,000.00	$5.12
Day 15	$150,000.00	$163.84
Day 20	$200,000.00	$5,242.88
Day 25	$250,000.00	$167,772.16
Day 30	$300,000.00	$5,368,709.12

A: The first option would add up to $300,000. It's true, this is a large amount of money. However, the second option would actually earn you more than $5 million!

Glossary

asset - something of value owned by a person, a business, or a government.

balance - the amount of money in a bank account.

corporation - a large business or organization made up of a group of people who have the legal right to act as one person.

debt (DEHT) - something owed to someone, especially money.

Great Depression - the period from 1929 to 1942 of worldwide economic trouble. There was little buying or selling, and many people could not find work.

inflation - a rise in the price of goods and services.

principal - the original amount someone invested, separate from earnings. Principal is also the amount borrowed or the amount still owed on a loan, separate from interest.

priority - the condition of coming before others, as in order or importance.

real estate - property, including buildings and land.

security - a document showing that someone owns or has invested in a company, an organization, or its stock. Also, something given as proof of a promise to make a payment later, especially a bond.

standard of living - the amount of wealth, comfort, and possessions that a person or group has.

stressful - full of or causing strain or pressure.

Web Sites

To learn more about the economy in action, visit ABDO Publishing Company online. Web sites about saving and investing are featured on our Book Links page. These links are routinely monitored and updated to provide the most current information available.

www.abdopublishing.com

Index